In the Breathing Time

BY

Linda C. Ehrlich

I would like to thank the visual artists for their inspiration and for their generous contributions to this book. The design work was greatly enhanced by the technical skill and artistry of Jared Bendis and Corey Wright.

“A Walk in the Magic Garden” was inspired by the photographs of Czech photographer Josef Sudek.

“Haru Kaze” was inspired by a woodblock print by Uchima Ansei

“Cuando los pájaros duermen” was inspired by the painting of the same name by Cuban painter Gina Pellón.

“Blossoming Jasmines” was inspired by the musical composition of the same name by Latvian composer Georgs Pelēcis.

Shika Press

ISBN 978-0-9858786-0-3

This book is dedicated to my brother Marty, the music man.

PREVIOUSLY PUBLISHED

"Chikubushima Island/Japan March 2011" was published in *The Bitter Oleander* (Fall 2011)

"Kagemusha," inspired by the Japanese film of the same name, was published online in *Puppetry International* (26, special issue on Shadow Puppetry, Fall/Winter 2009: 17).

"A Walk in the Magic Garden" and "Mai Po Marshes" were published in *The Bitter Oleander* 13:1 (Spring 2007).

"The Wind´s Impression," "Mekong Delta Journey," and "Haru Kaze (Spring Rain)" were published in *Tributaries* (Spring 2004).

"Cades Cove" was published in the *Southern Poetry Review* (Summer 1994).

"The Gulf"was published in the *International Poetry Review* (Spring 1992).

"Orpheus" was published in the *Case Reserve Review* (1988-89), and "Chinatown," and "Houseboat" in the Spring 1990 issue.

"Braille," and "Foreigner" were published in *Literary Arts Hawaii* (#91, 1989).

ILLUSTRATIONS

Flight: Inspired by Carol Holmes by Susan Griffith - Cover photograph

Original Print to accompany "Sculpture Garden" by Susanna Harris - 12

Original print to accompany "Crab Hunting" by Susanna Harris - 34

Notturno (mezzotint, maniera nera, 2002) by Enrico Della Torre - 44

Himeiji Castle (photo-illustration) by Jared Bendis - 68

Original drawing to accompany "Mekong Delta Journey" by Jane McChesney - 88

Original drawing by Cliff McChesney - 100

Untitled (mezzotint, maniera nera, 2002) by Enrico Della Torre - 120

Veduta di Genova dal Righi (acquaforte e acquatinta) Paola Ginepri. (Courtesy of the Galleria San Bernardo, Genoa Italy, and the artist) - 130

Original drawing by Cliff McChesney - 139

All illustrations courtesy of the artists

TABLE OF CONTENTS

Sculpture Garden

Sculpture Garden	13
Calder's Mobile	15
Braille	17
Gold	19
A Walk in the Magic Garden	21
Color-Field	23
Arab Market	25
For Richard Brautigan	27
Emily Dickinson	29
Orpheus	31
The Wind's Impression	33
Crab Hunting	35
Cades Cove	37
Mount Mitchell	39
Houseboat	41
Bride Behind the Trees	43
Full Moon Evening	45
Ballad	47
Pietà Rondanini	49
Milestones	51

Asia Journeys

Chikubushima Island / Japan March 2011	54
Mai Po Marshes	57
The Arbor / Tiananmen Square	59
Outlines / Chinese Proverb	61
Foreigner	63
House of the Sleeping Beauties	65
Meiji	67
White Crane Fortress (Himeijijo)	69
Ameagari (After the rain)	71
Kookam	73
Haru Kaze (Spring Wind)	75
Round-Leafed Willow (Hiroshima)	76
Chinatown	79
The Dalai Lama's Laughter	81
Istanbul	83
Full Moon Rising	85
Devi	87
Mekong Delta Journey	89
Kagemusha (The Shadow Warrior)	91
Miroku Bosatsu	93

Better Peace

Lullaby	97
Not the Real Words	99
Memorial Day (2009)	101
Bartering Survivors	103
To the Woman Next Door	105
The Gulf	107
Stones	109
Fortress	111
Euridice	113
Shells (Calafell)	115
To the Man with Green Eyes	117
Praise	119
Night Harbour	121
To the Child Who Loves Nests	123
Cuando Los Pájaros Duermen	125
Blossoming Jasmine	126
Manatee	129
New Language	131
Ligurian Ballad	133
Moorings	135
Beginnings	137

SCULPTURE GARDEN

SCULPTURE GARDEN

Close to the breast
the heart flutters

rising
as seven sparrows—

        Dragons of autumn—

brushing the angular leaves.

CALDER'S MOBILE

Five red arcs
with their shadow of jade

like a question

balanced

        in the beveled air

Braille

Only one word is needed
to descend
a dream of moving stairs

like
moonlight
trapped behind the pier.

Only one word born
of pale, brittle petals

girded in roses
and steel.

GOLD

In the house of masks, any face will do.

The one that you wear to speak the truth but, failing,
smile.

The one pinned against the wall.

In the house of masks, the gold one speaks, bending
like a leaf before the flame.

A Walk In The Magic Garden

A whole egg in a glass
like a nude
shining
in the darkness.

A head resting
against an oval stone.

And inside the rain-streaked window,

        memory itself

rises
like a feather
in the air.

COLOR-FIELD

in memory of Camille Claudel

Women carved from marble
are offered chisels without handles,

baskets of oranges
and wine.

Women carve in
                    silence

                              Monumental

          unfinished nudes.

ARAB MARKET

The labyrinth is long, and dark at either end.
Smiling men hold out tasseled shawls for you.
Dusty children wait at your feet.

Night, but you go out.

Dim lights from cobbled backstreets
have carried away the stars.

The labyrinth is long and dark at either end.

A blind child offers her hand.

For Richard Brautigan*

on his death by suicide

The river you sifted through your fingers
        to gills and sand,

like that first bird of morning
that called you from sleep.

        (Sweet Monday
        barbarous
        with cloves)

That river
you sifted through your fingers

drowns us
with skylines,

dark jesters,

night.

*author of *Trout Fishing in America*

Emily Dickinson

Emily Dickinson alone in her house after her father died. How the silence must have lengthened the days...the trees outside the windows, the restless flowers all became friends, as did the Day and her sister, Night, and the great frost of Death arriving in a carriage to carry her out into sound.

Orpheus

Ascended from darkness

the ten-headed demon
behind
glass trees.

Ascending,
        blind to the moment passing,

the shadow
of strings.

THE WIND'S IMPRESSION

Hakone Sculpture Garden, Japan

Late into the night
cries of street vendors
pierce
the cold mountain air.

I lie awake
beside
the man's sleeping form--

recumbent Buddhas
lost to each other.

How can we comprehend such sounds?

    Melancholy echo
    of words
    never to be spoken.

Lost languages of the wind
remain

    resistant to change.

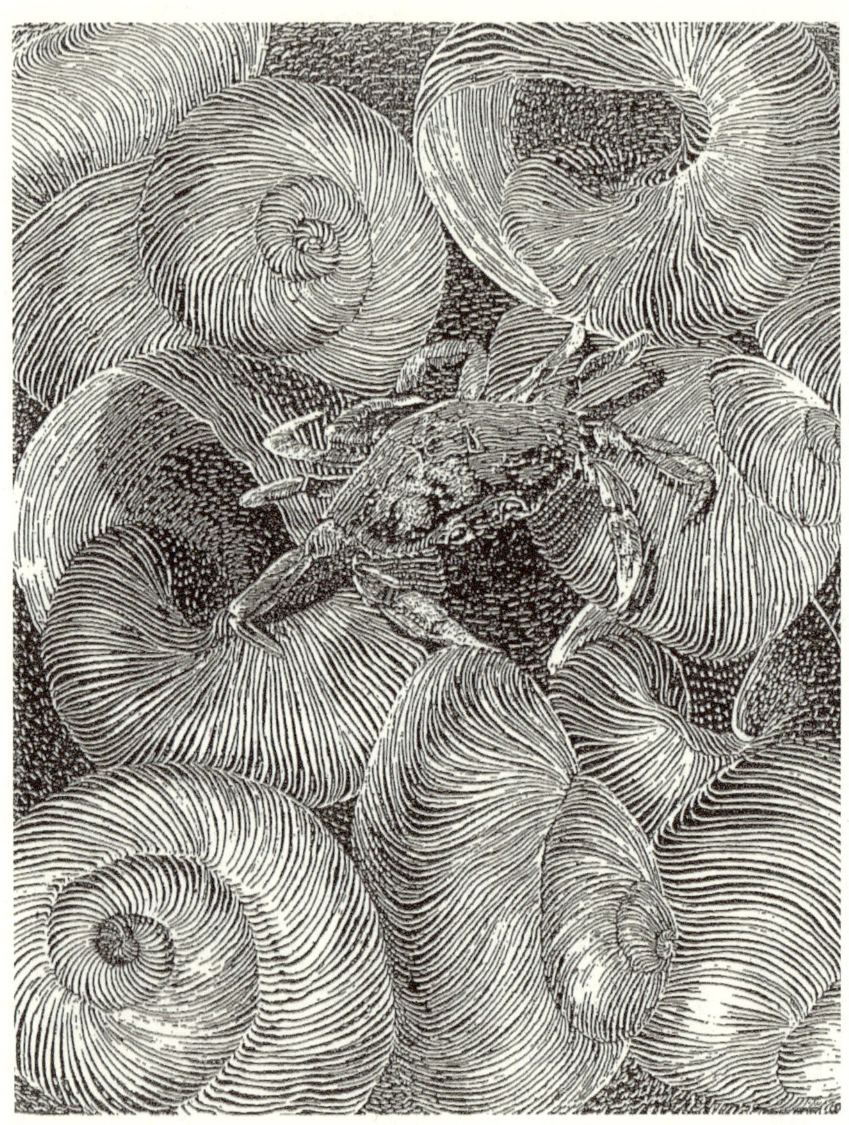

Crab Hunting

Every seven years
the lunar clowns,
oval with silence,
cast circles of light onto the sands.

        I must change my life.

Images
        seductive
float before me

like pale, iridescent shells.

Cades Cove

Tuckaleechee Caverns,
home of the spinning river,
the steadfast pine.

The one
with love
dammed up
like a stream full of leaves.

Tuckaleechee Caverns—

        to seek such comfort
        from your body—

Home of the spinning river,
the steadfast pine.

Mount Mitchell

Salamander branches
from trees that will not rot

on top of Mount Mitchell.

The smallest insect
mixed with grey rain
eats away at the dry landscape.

(We sell our children to the highest bidder)

What is left for us
now
but a furious compassion?

Branches
the color of burnt shells,

and evergreens
farther
below.

HOUSEBOAT
Paul Klee

Beneath the lake

lucent
skeletons of fish

        and the sharp teeth of combs—

                an eye dislocated—

        and creatures who weep red tears.

Bride Behind The Trees

on the death of Marc Chagall

White-gloved men
behind Evening's green form

await the striking
of the monstrous bell,

and cows
kneaded
from mountains.

Enter with autumn.

Enter inverted

against
a wedding's noon.

Full Moon Evening

Evening with you.
Harbour of burning leaves.

I return to a lighted room.

In your arms
I become an island
of dark majestic birds.

Faint melody
captured by water,
carried by wind.

You have stolen the moon
and poured it like quicksilver
through my veins.

Echo of my silence,
Evening with you.

Ballad

Now that you have returned to me
the warmth of arcs,

Song of a dove lost
among white porcelain.

Now that you have breathed in me
new sounds
soft as smoke
rising
across a field of ancient hearths.

The night opens

furiously

with stars, my love

Now
that you have returned.

Pietà Rondanini

Michelangelo's last sculpture

Half-standing, half-leaning
        unfinished
                mother and child   emerge
                from the callous stone,

the welcoming stone.

But I flee
from the Enormity
of unrequited gravity,

        Tenderness

chiseled out of air.

MILESTONES

I had always heard there were signs
hidden
in the forest,

branches
half-bent back in the wind,

three-hundred-year old Sequoyahs
whose rings
tell stories

difficult to decipher.

Now that we have reached
years
of round numbers,

Signs
rise up   before us
like stones
smoothed
          by the river's run.

We step over them
          lightly,
without looking down.

Asia Journeys

CHIKUBUSHIMA

Japan - March 2011

You have to take it both ways.

The Dragon King with his fiery orange mane,
and the lilac goddess with her pale silk robes.

On that island surrounded by placid ripples
stoic ducks
ride out the Winter,
        their red heads bobbing above the water.

Surviving.

You have to take it both ways.

The earth shakes
and gobbles whole villages in a flash.

        Pray to the Dragon King to protect us.
        Pray to the Goddess of Wisdom to guide us.

Ducks on Lake Biwa
know that Spring is in the air.

They keep to themselves
and stay away from noisy seagulls
who happen to find themselves on that shore.

First the Lilac Goddess emerges from her shelter.
Then the Dragon King kicks his heels,
        spraying a huge wall of water.

Stand on the gentle shore
and gaze out at Chikubushima.

As nice as it might be to climb the stairs
to the sacred island shrine,

you´d probably have to pass by row after row
of cheap tourist shops
along the way.

Mai Po Marshes

Hong Kong 1998

We travel halfway around the world
to watch black butterflies
cross
barbed wire
        without permits,

and morning glories
twist free
through hoops of steel.

On the border
of China

we stand, gazing at mangroves
receding,

while white egrets
rise
from the sand.

The Arbor

Tiananmen Square

In the shadow of days,
child at breast,
sparrow at wing.

One man standing
before a row of tanks
is a thousand men

                    standing.

One tired bird
takes flight,

and the leaves are set free.

OUTLINES

Chinese Proverb

Earth pulls at the moon
and mist rises

across a lake of stone,
an ocean of fire.

Woman is water,
Man is clay.

Water softens metal.
Metal gives water form.

From this distance
I can recall
the outline of your face

like a planet
lost in its own orbit,

playing with the tides.

Foreigner

Like a small child
sent out to a field
to test for mines

I have no past or future.

Flowers do not cling to me.

Now in midwinter
as copper leaves descend
I wait

watched by a hundred wooden eyes.

House Of The Sleeping Beauties

a visit to Kawabata Yasunari's house

The same black cat still waits
among the cedars
alone
as that severed bronze hand
on the low writing table

        and why—

staring out at the bottomless garden,
out at those grave markers from Korean wells,

Why turn away?

        (woman revealed in the nodes of bamboo)

--this madness.

Meiji

Gardenias in the moonlight
beside the Emperor's shrine.

Fragrance,
of a forgotten splendor.

I take your hand,

the closed moment of your skin.

White blossoms,
faint traces,

guarded
by soldiers
in Imperial brown.

WHITE CRANE FORTRESS
Himejijo

Alone/ as if a castle with paper walls were standing

unguarded, and yet standing

and moving

        like a white bird
                        asymmetrically

Ameagari

after the rain

After the rain
        long-haired girls
tiptoe
arm-in-arm
past oily puddles,

moats
of a moment's fortress.

Frogs' cries
through river-blown reeds
cross the rain fields

rising.

KOOKAM*

On the night Venus and Jupiter
align,

a star of zero magnitude
floods
my body
with light.

        This is how it begins—

        a crossed handshake,
                the dropping of coins.

You enter the new town in a torrential downpour.
A town of houses hidden in trees.

        This is how it begins.

On the night when the horseman of Heaven
links two stars

I walk out alone
by the river
        with you at my side.

* A Thai expression for a man and woman who are destined to be with each other.

Haru Kaze
Spring Wind

In blocks of blue and white
a breeze passes.

Winter passes.

        I step over suitcases on the stairs.

In sharp dashes of gold and lilac
        you enter my life

like a black mountain inverted,

like a Spring wind.

Round-Leafed Willow

Hiroshima

Mountains beyond mountains in the blue-shade morning but still

gnarled
round-leafed
willow

spreading out its leaves
to catch the light
that calm August morning

before the sky ended.

City of ashes

Rivers of fire

But still you stood.

What stairway descends from your stubborn roots
        to the molten eye at the Earth's center?

Round-leafed willow--
hibakusha survivor.

        Loving hands have filled your wounds
        with healing balm

                so you remain today

                full of grace.

Only angels and children
hear your cries

but they sing a song
too sweet
for your burnt-out ears.

Chinatown

Seed pearls
and red-skinned chickens
hung up to dry

in fantastic marriages.

        Chinatown—

Sailors wander down
calligraphic alleys

and Vietnamese mothers
wrapped in steam

crowd the mosaic doorways
and spill out to the streets.

THE DALAI LAMA'S LAUGHTER

An exhalation, churning of the ocean. "Light,"
some might say, and truly he is, this Buddhist
monk with the great laugh.

While the Chinese turn his country into a cheap
theme park, he refuses a boycott of Chinese goods
because it would hurt the poor who make them.

Twelve steps ahead of us and then he returns, a
myriad smiles on his lips.

Smile of agony, smile of resignation, smile of
delight.

Istanbul

Still life in the sultan's summer palace, in a city
that keeps shifting before my eyes.

First you are grey stone, and then golden light.
Plain working brown,

and then rococo jewel.

I cannot recall your name. Your name is mosque.
Your name is mosaic

in a sea of green.

Istanbul! this whisper that we are

whirls in circles,

not knowing if our feet stay on the ground.

Full Moon Rising

Radiance of a black pearl,

the full moon rising.

Full moon lingering
until morning
in the clear autumn sky.

We have dipped into the well of Heaven
to draw up clear water.

We await the New Year.

Devi

Ponderous mother
carved from stone

or henna-hand mother
draped in red silk.

This time I am alone with India.

Alone with the wheels of gods
whirling off into space.

And what has become of that half-blind child,

and the farmer
who offered to share his tea with me
beside a fire in the field?

Mekong Delta Journey

outside Ho Chi Minh City

I would like to lie down and sleep in Vietnam,
shaded by banana leaves,

washed by a sudden tropical rain.

I would like to lie down in dark, muddy fields
        guarded
                by the graves of ancestors

        as green rice plants rise
        over long abandoned battlefields.

I would like to lie down and sleep in Vietnam
while the jungle reclaims the years.

KAGEMUSHA
The Shadow Warrior

A thief, yet he looks like a lord.
          (Yellow sun, centered in a red sky)

Children and animals can tell the difference,
          still the double takes chances.

Shadow of the shadow,
there can be no mistakes.

When the shadow warrior takes up his banner,
real men fall in battle.

Riderless horses rush forward
in a landscape of carnage.

Draped in white, the shadow warrior watches

                    helpless.

He alone tastes victory
or its shadow   which is the same.

Miroku Bosatsu

Kyoto, Japan

Buddha of the future

What delicate line
        lies just below the horizon?

With your upraised hand
        guide miniature warriors
        through childhood's fury.

Miroku Bosatsu!

Teach us how to chart our course
        with lines of fire

across Evening's great divide.

Better Peace

LULLABY

I would accept peace in any form--

as a wrinkled old woman,
or the last black swan.

I would take her in my arms
and sing lullabies until she sleeps.

I would accept peace
as a corner in a crowded station
reserved
for fine ladies and women of the night.

Let peace flow like a swift rushing river

or like the whisper
of an ancient buried stream.

NOT THE REAL WORDS

It takes a system
to kill a large number of people.

Everything must be orderly,
hidden,
as quick as possible,
as clean as possible,

so that all that remains are the stones.

And stones
need no description.

Memorial Day (2009)

Exhibit A.
We put our wounded on display.

Exhibit B.
Question wrong
but answer right.

Young men explode
across a desert floor.

Exhibit war
(and Hooray!)

Exhibit night,

dignity
and shattered light.

BARTERING SURVIVORS

What started out whole
comes back
as small change.

What started out round
returns
with edges.

    Weary,
    I laid my head against a stone,
    and heard its murmuring retreat

unravel
through my fingers

to ash.

THE WOMAN NEXT DOOR
en route to Egypt and Israel

The woman next door
wakes up as we do,
watching the sun enter the window

handcuffed to a wall
for three days.

The woman next door
behind bullet-proof glass
smiles
at the men who enter without knocking,
whose hands become ice.

        Better peace than land.
        Better peace than the memory of land.

See how her children flee
from those hallowed stones,
        ancient sanctuaries,
                fields of glass.

The woman next door
bakes bread over a flame

and her hands overflow with light.

THE GULF

We made love at the outbreak of war.

Tanks rolled over our skin
and the residue of longing
exploded,
scattering soft ashes.

Like the tears of war
we crossed borders.

Missiles
without targets.

The finest radar at rest.

STONES

"Stone is enduring time" (Osamu Noguchi)

What do they tell us, all these worn stones?

Amazed frescoes with their mouths ajar
reclaimed
by the twisted roots of trees.

    If we lean our foreheads
        against an ancient wall,

    If we kneel down
        at the feet of angels,

    If we cover our head
        at the call to prayer,

will the stones soak up
all this wasted blood

        (soldiers
        returned
        as loose coins)

and grant us peace?

Fortress

All forts should be ruins
crumbling under the hot August sun.

All guns,
relics.

    There is nowhere to sit
    in Fort Sumter

and the flags make a racket in the wind.

EURIDICE

If the gates are lifted,
why do these shadows
block my way?

Be for me eyes

        and path

        and echo.

Do not turn to look
where love's madness has led us,
                    gazing at specters.

    Why do I need your words of comfort?

    Why do you need my blindness?

SHELLS

Calafell

It is my duty to collect shells while wars rage far across the ocean. Useless shells and rocks smoothed down by the waves. It is my duty to sit by these seven palm trees while families with baby carriages promenade by.

Far from the waves of war. As dogs with donkey ears and fast-talking bicyclists speed by.

My duty it is to gather shells, eyes of Vishnu, and rocks smoothed down by this tideless sea. Each nautilus shell is a reminder of those living. Each *megadama*-shaped rock, a refusal to give war any prominence, any inevitability.

My solemn duty to gather useless shells by this turquoise sea.

To the Man with Green Eyes

In the garden of white roses
you awake,
marble sculptures poised at your side,

young man with the crystal green eyes.

What do you see inside yourself,
eyes the color of ripe fields in July?

    Imagine yourself a phosphorescent creature
    on the ocean floor,

    or a coalblack bird with white wings.

Imagine yourself in a courtyard of fountains
    far from the scaffolding of night.

In the uncertain dawn
you awake
by the blinding scarlet bougainvillea.

And what do you see inside of me,

    young man with the seagreen eyes?

Praise

Praise the Lord with the bird hovering
over a still pool of water,

rain sliding suddenly off the roof.

Praise with the cessation of rain.

Night Harbour

Our words, suspended
over a sea of mirrors

like five long-tailed kites
floating in unison

against the flow of stars.

To The Child Who Loves Nests

A child
trails a cloth behind her,

long shawl of red and green rivers.

Before the tired eyes
of grown-up mountaineers

a child drapes herself in feathers,
swaying
to a ten-year-old samba.

May the world—
        even this brittle world—
cushion you
in soft grasses.

        May you dance in ever-widening circles.

                May it catch you
                when you fall.

Cuando Los Pájaros Duermen

When the birds sleep,
my child
gathers her iridescent wings around her

and sleeps

like those women whose blue claws
grasp branches,

whose orange-feathered headdresses
stream out behind them
in the sun.

When the birds dream,
my child wraps her rainbow form
gently
around herself

and rests.

Blossoming Jasmine

Flecks of the moon

these blossoming jasmine

suddenly
rooted

and yet floating,
soaring

in nights of draped slumber.

Tell me of worlds I have never seen
   in languages I can only imagine.

Tell me of harbours
where boats leave quietly out to sea
at dawn

and return with incense from Damascus,
   fragrant tea from China,

garlands of pikake flowers from the Hawaiian islands,

jasmine oil from India.

Tell me of vines

full

of fallen stars

so delicate

even the faintest breath will blow them away.

Listen!

cascades of jasmines

are playing a melody

on silent chimes.

Manatee

Boulder of the sea.

A mother manatee
caresses her young

and floats
free

through perilous waters.

Stillness in motion/

        motion
        in stillness.

Silver
outlined in white.

New Language

We watch as a pelican
hovers
over the water,

diving straight down
for its prey.

Now we are learning a new language.

Morning follows night

(Soft night of lost mirrors)

The song I could not sing
sings in your eyes.

A pelican circles.

It gathers its wings.

Ligurian Ballad

All the old stories have been forgotten.
Now there is only the ocean
to cover us

at the end of day.

Cheap treasures
set out for sale
in the market.

Now we have only the sun
to bargain with

at the end of day.

All the old terrors have been forgotten.
Now there is only the wind
to welcome us

at the end of the sheltered day.

All the old memories have been forgotten.
Now only the wings of the gull
remind us

at the end of the endless day.

MOORINGS

The measure of a harbor
is in its shadow.

Measure of love
in its shelter.

The measure of a drum
is in its moorings.

Our measure

in our song.

BEGINNINGS

Angels of bridges,

Angels of damask and grain.

The one who pulls small children
away from fires.

Angels draped in egret feathers,

and the one who directed you to me,
        across a frozen lake
        in the breathing time.

www.ingramcontent.com/pod-product-compliance
Lightning Source LLC
LaVergne TN
LVHW091002080826
845145LV00003B/1101

* 9 7 8 0 9 8 5 8 7 8 6 0 3 *